THE COVER-UP

A Satirical Mystery

By Pierre LeBlanc

Portions of this book were gleaned from the files at CIA, under the rules and regulations of the Freedom of Information Act. We disclaim all authenticity for such information, and in no way do we agree or disagree with the information disclosed in this white paper.

Cajun Intelligence Administration
Toulous Letrec, Asst. Director

Written and translated by George Marti

Pierre LeBlanc is the pen name of George Marti

Illustrations by Taama Marti Forasiepi

First editions published by Delpetro Corporation in 1991

INTRODUCTION

“Son,” say Uncle Boudreaux, “you ask me, ‘what is a politician?’ Now to answer that question you have to define what a politician do. Take our Congressman Bulgebottom for example. What he do up there in Washington is vote for tax laws, to take money from one people, and give that money he take to other people. The first people is very unhappy ‘cause he take his money away, and the second people is unhappy ‘cause they didn’t get enough. Now a politician is a man that can keep both of those peoples happy enough to vote for him come next election. Our Congressman Bulgebottom is just that kind a man. He be representing us Bayou folks for nigh on thirty five year. As one famous American say, ‘Politics is a tricky game, played by tricky people.’ ”

CHAPTER 1

"Son, you talk about the income tax. Now your grandpa spoke of it when they first pass that law. He say to me, 'Ignace, I don't believe in that tax, and I'm not going to sign up for any of it.' "

Pierre listened to Uncle Boudreaux's tax philosophy, while he sopped up the remnants of his sauce piquant with the heel of his French bread. Leaning back in his chair, he turned to his Uncle Boudreaux, "When we go up there to Washington, are they going to double talk us about the take-over of the Lafite Savings?"

Pierre's uncle, Ignace Boudreaux, a self-made man and considered the entire length of Bayou Barataria, as the most astute business man in Bayou Country, smiled at his nephew's question.

"Pierre, I've been asked by the depositors of Lafite Savings to get to the bottom of this serious problem, and I don't plan to let no double talk stand in the way.

"You know, I done advised many my friend to put their money in Lafite Savings, even my ole friend Jacque Shopper, he done let the Lafite Savings finance his strip shoppin' center, and that represent one of the main incomes the Lafite Savings have to pay the people in their saving accounts.

"Now the regulators come say all the capital has disappeared, poof, out the window. Only place to find out the true fact is to go direct to Washington D.C., where all those experts stay."

"But how we going to get in to see all those important people Uncle Boudreaux?"

"You done forget yourself boy, your Uncle am the editor of the Lafite Weekly Lagniappe, and as such, a newspaper man entitled to the same respect, and privilege, as the editor of that Washington Post."

"We going to get you started on your political indoctrination right here and now. Com' on let's get rest up, tomorrow is one long fly to the Capitol."

Following the hour drive from Lafite to New Orleans International airport, Uncle Boudreaux and Pierre, settled back in their plane seats as the engines began to rev up. While Pierre busied himself with a picture magazine, purchased at the airport news stand, Ignace was engaged in making notes on the avenues of enquiry he had dictated to Susie Teriot, his secretary, the previous day. As he thought of Susie, his full time Secretary and part time good time friend, Ignace drifted off into a reminisce of the pleasures they had shared in and out of the office, for the past ten years.

He was jolted out of his reverie by Pierre's

insistent nudging of his elbow. "Who we going to see first, Uncle Boudreaux?"

"Son, we going to see the man that has been the political backbone of the Bayou Country for the past thirty-five year. A man of great integrity, a man who represent the very essence of everything near and dear to us folks down on the Bayou, Congressman, Bulgebottom."

As the plane circled in its Washington holding pattern, Boudreaux reflected, "Pierre, see those clouds covering that Washington?"

"Shore do." replied Pierre. "Well son," say Boudreaux, "sometime we can see them, and sometime we can't, but to the residents of this place, they always there, and in the middle of those clouds is a big glass dome that houses everyone and everything in Washington."

Boudreaux shifted in his seat and continued

his discourse, "Now when you first come here, a man can see right through that big Bingo Dome, but then 'incumbent-itis' begins to set in, and after eight, ten years the glass and the clouds forms a big reflector that reflects all of the information passing back and forth inside the dome, kinda like the plastic balls at the Lafite Church bingo game."

"Yes sir, son, that 'incumbent-itis' gets to be a very serious disease. I've got a feeling in my bones, when we get to nosin' around, we're going to find that ole 'incumbent- itis' have something to do with the disappearance of the capital from Lafite Savings."

"Can't say I understand what you're talking about Uncle," says Pierre.

"Remember when we came up here a few years back, when I was the roving reporter for the Lafite Lagniappe?" Pierre remembered well the trip, and especially his uncle's encounter with the Roving

Canal Street reporter from the New Orleans WPMB station. The day before they take the plane to Washington, Uncle had been showing Pierre around the city, and explaining how she all built below sea level, with those big levee, and those big pumps a man could drive a truck into. They pump every drop of rain water out of the city. Up river they have those big flood gates, that open when the Mississippi get on a rampage, and dump the ole Mississippi into Lake Pontchartrain, so's the city folks won't be up to their rear end in water, should those levee break.

"Well sir," say the Roving Canal Street Interviewer, collaring Uncle Boudreaux, "what do you think of the Watergate Affair?"

Uncle kinda hesitated and pondered, you could see the idea form as it popped into his head, and out of his mouth simultaneously, "Man," say Uncle Boudreaux, "they open those gates, it's sure going to ruin the shrimpin' and crabbin' in the lake."

Most of the crowd on Canal Street agreed with Uncle, but that announcer had his tongue in his mouth sideways a good minute, before he could quit laughing.

Looking back, I could understand the announcer's problem, cause I heard later, he had just come to New Orlins. But I say to Uncle, "What's Watergate have to do with 'incumbent-itis?' "

"Well son, think of it this way, four or five men break into an office, which has no valuables and no secrets, bent on stealing the contents. So our President, being a long time Washingtonian, and an incumbent to boot, does the natural thing. He recognize that no politician can admit a mistake by hisself, or anyone in his camp, so he try to cover up the connection. Now the talk bounces around the Washington Bingo Dome, until the noise become downright deafening. First thing you know, those Washingtonians at each other like ten of cousin Petout's fighting cocks, in a tag team bout."

"Meanwhile," continued Uncle, "the rest of us are all sitting on the outside of the Bingo Dome hoping they get on with the countries business, and wondering what the hell all the commotion are about? This was a perfect example of ole 'incumbent-itis' disease at work."

"Remember the stories about the Hatfields and the Coys up there in those hills?" continued Uncle, "they had a form of 'incumbent-itis' just like those D.C. 'ins. The hills insulate them, just like the Bingo Dome insulate those Washingtonians, and they get so entrenched in their thinking, that there's no flexibility left in 'em. The rest of us have a mighty hard time figuring out, what they all a fighting and a feuding about."

CHAPTER 2

The door to Representative Bulgebottom‘s office hit Pierre on the rear, as it closed on him and Boudreaux. “Miss,” say Uncle, “Boudreaux, from the Lafite Lagniappe, to see the Congressman immediately. We have a private meeting scheduled for 9 a.m.”

“Of course,” purred the secretary, “have a seat gentlemen.”

Uncle Boudreaux really knew how to impress these Capitol folks. Around 3 p.m. in comes this dapper little fellow, with ascot and spats and an exceptionally wide posterior. He don’t ask nobody nothin’, nor do the six folks, who come behind him. They shore must have been important citizens, cause they walked right into Congressman Bulgebottom’s office without a whimper from that dicy little blonde secretary. Didn’t seem fair to me, so I say to Uncle Boudreaux, “How come they get to go ahead of us?"

Uncle Boudreaux was a thinking strong on this, I could tell, 'cause his eye brows start to pump up and down, like they was cranking some important knowledge into his brain cells. Finally he says, "Can't be sure 'cause Buldgebottom hasn't been back to Cajun country for twenty years, but that first fellow sure did resemble him. Maybe it was one of his brothers. Could be his brother Cal, the one that collected the Bulgebottom election fees." Then Uncle must have changed his mind, 'cause he said, "No couldn't be Cal, he still in state prison at Angola."

Along about 5 p.m. the buzzer rings, and in we go for our meeting. The secretary whispers on the way in, "We usually close at five, but the Congressman is making an exception for the representative of the press." Like I said, Uncle Boudreaux was an important man.

“Mon ami,” exclaims the ascot and spats man, “it is always a pleasure to see close friends from the Bayou.” Ascot give Uncle a big hug and smile.

Uncle Boudreaux is so modest, didn’t mention what old friends he was with the Congressman, “Sit, sit,” the second sit, I decided was for me, so uncle and I sat. I was kinda looking around, and that spats man, who by now looked like he must be Congressman Bulgebottom in the flesh, must a been watching our every move, cause he says, “Don’t mind my assistants, they are part of the trusted team here, working for the folks back home.” One of the team was 38-24-36, she could be on my team anytime.

Uncle Boudreaux, he gets right to the point, “The regulators closed down the Lafite Savings.” “What!, Why?” exclaims Bulgebottom.

Uncle turns to me, and I say, “The capital disappeared.”

"Nonsense son," replies Bulgebottom, "Baton Rouge is still there."

"No sir," I says, "the Federal Regulators getting ready to close down Lafite Savings, 'cause they say its capital has disappeared." The Congressman opened the bottom drawer, where it looked like he kept his supply of "Bayou Water," and had a long draught. You could tell he'd been a Bayou jug man at one time. "Who stole the money?" questioned Bulgebottom, "we'll get the Attorney General on this right away." From the tone of his voice, I knew we now had his full attention.

Then Uncle Boudreaux chimed in, "The depositors committee done asked me to come here and find out how this could happen."

"Happen! happen!" Bulgebottom's blood pressure headed in an upward spiral, "How could you expect me to know who the thief was?" This statement kinda surprised me, 'cause Uncle

Boudreaux hadn't mentioned any thieves, but then these folks in Washington knew everything.

Uncle had the fish on the hook, and he was a master at reeling them in, so he decides he's going to do away with this local thief concept right now.

"There's only three peoples can write checks at the Lafite Savings. Uncle Jamie, he's 94 now and can't see well enough to make his mark anymore, and no one has Touche Le Plume for him. Then there's Father Donovan, he's a director, and then there was your brother Silas, but as you know, Silas done died dead a few years back, and your Mama temporarily took his place." This looked to me like a mystery for Inspector Clouseau, or maybe that Attorney General, Congressman Bulge-bottom mentioned earlier.

The Congressman's red nose appreciably reddened, and his squeaky eyes narrowed even further, then after a few moments reflection, he advises, "Don't worry Bilteau," missing uncle's name, "this must be a clerical error by the district regulators. I'll speak to the Chief Regulator myself." You could see he had formulated a plan. "You gentlemen spend the rest of the day looking over our great Capitol, head on back to the Bayou, and leave this knotty little problem to your Representative."

Turning to his assistant, who looked to be Bulgebottom's caretaker for 38-24-36, Bulgebottom snapped, "John, show these fine folks from back home around the city, and make sure they make it to their plane in plenty of time. Mary," he calls to the dicy one, "Mary, make sure our friends have confirmed reservations for early tomorrow morning. Tell them Congressman Bulgebottom wants his friends to have priority preference. Yes sir, Boteau," missing Uncle's name another hair, "you tell those voters back home, what good care we take of our friends, when they come to the

Capitol."

It seems we were leaving. John edged us out to the outer office, and motioned to a fellow named Phil who hustled us down the elevator, where we were introduced to Joe, who took us by the Washington D.C., McDonalds, a fancy one, where Uncle Boudreaux bought us all a hamburger, then we saw the rest of Washington in the cab ride back to the hotel.

We folks from the Bayou turn out just before cock crows, so I'm up and ready to head for the airport, but Uncle Boudreaux has me down the back stairs, and out the rear door, which must be a short cut to the airport. After about two hours of meandering around the park, and twenty phone calls by Uncle Boudreaux, I find us at this big building with people running from somewhere to nowhere as fast as they can trot. Uncle Boudreaux explained, that these folks were carrying the twelve shredder drafts of the memos for approval by the recipient, prior to the final file copy, which would be filed once the drafts were approved by the recipient and sender.

In Lafite, we'd just walk next door and tell folks what we had on our mind, but that didn't seem to be the method for the really important papers, that passed back and forth here in the Capitol. Course it sure did make a need for a lot of good jobs for folks. Maybe that's what we need in Lafite, for the folks who look like they going to lose their jobs at Lafite Savings.

Uncle Boudreaux takes a look at the directory, and off we go to the 12th floor. This fella at the 12th floor wants to know, "Who you looking for?" Uncle tells him, "Mr. Charm, the Chief Regulator."

"May I see your appointment slip?" Uncle Boudreaux then flashes his Press Card and says, "Press interview."

The fellow gets on the phone and chats a minute, then he says, "You go to the fourth floor, room 4567, desk 734, they'll take care of you." Off we go to the fourth floor, and in less than an hour and forty minutes, we come up to room 4567, and in another thirty-five minutes, we are standing in front of Desk 734. Unlike the scurrying in the halls, there wasn't much happening in room 4567. The man at Desk 734, looked like he didn't have a name, and I couldn't find the 734 on his forehead, although I felt sure it was going to be there someplace.

There weren't any extra chairs, so we stand, and 734 says, "Can I help you gentlemen?" I think Uncle Boudreaux smelled a detour, so he says, "We're looking for the Chief Regulator, Mr. Charm."

"Yes," replies this fellow, "I am one of Mr. Charm's special assistants, I'm sure I will be able to handle your problem."

What's to lose, so Uncle Boudreaux starts out, "We lost," and that was as far as he got.

"Sir," says 734, "you need to go to Room 5492, 5th floor, desk 586, and they will handle your problem promptly." Then he pick up the phone and start talkin' to Mildred.

We get to the 5th floor, but now it lunch time, and everyone is beelining it for the elevators, just like the stampede you see on the western TV show. Uncle Boudreaux and I slip in behind one of those large pillars, and in thirty minutes things calm down a bit, so's we can start looking for Room 5492. Uncle and I are learning fast, so in no time at all, we come onto 5492, and then right to desk 586. One look and I know as sure as a pack rat going to bring the goods home, that this is not Mr. Charm's desk, 'cause it say right on the sign "Lost and Found." This didn't seem to bother Uncle

Boudreaux, so he asks the man, “We lost the Lafite Savings capital, have you found it?”

“Humm,” say the fellow, as he searches his computer screen, “sorry sir, we have not found the Lafite Savings capital.”

Uncle almost double up with fun, looks at me and says, “Hear that Pierre, we know one thing for sure, that capital not hidden in that Washington computer.” Neither I nor number 586 could see much humor in the situation, but then Uncle Boudreaux was a man of the world.

This Mr. Charm is kinda like tracking a possum at night, he keep circling around so you lose the scent, so we head back to the first floor to reconnoiter.

Luck would have it, Uncle Boudreaux picks up the Washington Post, and right there on the front page it say, “Savings and Loan hearing, set for tomorrow. Senator Byall Means will chair the Joint House and Senate Committee hearing. Congressman Findmore Ways, whose mother was the daughter of the Long Island Findmore fortune will join Senator Means on the dais."

CHAPTER 3

Let me tell you, Uncle Boudreaux and I hit pay dirt at those Hearing. Up there on the Judgement panel, they have Senator Byall Means, Senator I.M. Taxwriter, that powerful Senator from New England, Senator Downtrodden, and of course representing the House of Representatives side, they had Congressman Findmore Ways. Seems our representative Bulgebottom didn't make the committee. Then I understand, they pick these folks on seniority, and our man Bulgebottom only been in Congress thirty-five years.

Later on I found out that Means, Taxwriter and Ways were the primary sponsors of the real estate portion of the 1986 tax revisions. Their bill picked up 15 billion dollars for the treasury, and didn't cost one vote. Based on Uncle Boudreaux's definition of a Politician, these fellows were certainly the "Masters of their trade."

We spent several weeks coming and going from those hearings, and if it hadn't been for those Senate and House Panel calling all those experts, Uncle Boudreaux and I wouldn't have known where to get started on looking for the Lafite capital.

They had a whole passel of experts. Right off the bat, they had Mr. Charm the Chief Regulator, then they had Cal Q. Later, he was the expert on the financial affairs of Savings & Loans, and then sometime later, they had these "Five Senators," who seemed to be right close to the financial institutions in the West.

They talk about some big, big, numbers. I can't count that high. Several hundred billion dollars seem to be missing, in addition to the $300,000 that was missing from Lafite Savings. As best we could make out, someone stole the money, just like Congressman Bulgebottom say, but it was kinda like the case of Lafite Savings, no one knew who, and how, they did the deed. Surely, they should call in Inspector Cousteau. Of course, at one point, the President said he was going to put the FBI to work on the case, and they going to put all the culprits in jail.

I couldn't take notes fast enough at those hearings, so we have Marie come up from Lafite to help us. Marie was fast with the pen, with a mystic bottom, and a genuine harassable top. Only defect Marie have is a brother, who play linebacker for the New Orlins Saints.

Long about the third week, Uncle Boudreaux decides to send Marie alone to the hearings, and he and I go looking for some expert we see testifying. It seem those expert who can talk about all those billions, should certainly be able to handle the Lafite Savings measly little $300,000 capital disappearance.

Uncle Boudreaux been mulling over in his mind, the expert who could put his finger right on the disappearance of the Lafite capital, and he come to the conclusion, this fellow Cal Q. Later is our man.

Turned out Cal Q. was holed up right at our Washington Hotel, not three floors away. Up we go to Mr. Cal Q's room and rap on the door. This Cal Q. must have felt left out, for he was more than delighted to talk to a member of the press. Cal Q. and Uncle Boudreaux hit it off right from the start. Seems Cal Q. had a sister that married a fellow Uncle knew in Lafayette.

After passing a few social words, Uncle broaches the subject. "We have a problem with the Lafite Savings, and I hear you testify before the committee that around 4% of the losses at the S&L's was due to mismanagement and downright stealing."

Uncle and I are getting really good with these initials, now that we been in D.C. so long.

"That's right," reply Cal Q.

Uncle gets out his pocket calculator and does a few quick numbers, and then he say, "Well at Lafite Savings, that seems to leave 96% of the funds disappear someplace else."

"It would seem that would be the case." says Cal Q. Then getting a little more businesslike in his tone, Cal Q. says, "our firm is the nation's foremost expert on S&Ls, and we certainly would be more than happy to send a team of our experts to Lafite to investigate the whereabouts of the remaining 96% of the missing capital at the Lafite Savings."

Uncle Boudreaux could not speak for Lafite Savings, but he say, "How many members on your expert team?"

Now Cal Q. zeros in, and you can see the dollar signs clicking in his eyes, "Maybe a ten man team could get the ball rolling."

Uncle Boudreaux was thinking this over, and I was counting. Let's see, Lafite Savings had Joe the teller, who also double as bookkeeper, Marie the part time secretary, the President and the two directors. There sure weren't enough chairs for any ten man team.

Uncle say, "Cal, would you have any small suggestions, as to where we might take a quick look ourselves for the 96%?"

"Mr. Boudreaux," now Cal was not so friendly, "we are a very professional organization, very thorough, we don't make suggestions."

Especially free suggestions, I thought.

On the way home in the cab, Uncle Boudreaux is deep in thought. It was hard for him to believe even 4% of the money had been mismanaged or stolen. All the cash was right there in the vault accounted for to the penny.

We seemed to be running into brick walls at every tum, and I was getting to feel like Uncle Boudreaux's Dr. Watson.

Nevertheless, we begin to feel our way along especially Uncle Boudreaux, who seemed to quite happy about the notes Marie had been taking at the hearing, so he says, "Pierre, you, me, and Marie off to see Representative Findmore Ways, then maybe we can tackle Senator Byall Means. Those two fine gentlemen done write the Ways Means tax reform act of 1986. If anyone understand, where our capital disappear, they are the ones."

Next morning, we three head for Congressman's Findmore Ways office, where we have the pleasure of spending the next three days reading magazines and letters to constituents. Marie and I are ready to give it up, but Uncle say it's just like stalking a leading buck deer, you've got to stay in the blind and bide your time.

The fourth day in come Findmore Ways, a lady's man if ever lamped one. Looks like Uncle spotted this characteristic in the animal at the hearing, and decided to tote Marie along. Ways takes one look at Marie, does a retake, and says to his secretary, "Show the lady in." The Secretary leans over and whispers, "Those gentlemen are with the young lady." The Congressman takes a third pass on Marie and smiling, "Of course and her two friends."

Now Congressman Ways has some fancy inner office, so we all have a seat and this neat little lady comes by and offers us a coffee or other refreshment. Ways puts the silver smile on Marie and says, "I'm Congressman Ways. I passed in such a hurry, I missed your name."

Now Marie was a little flustered, since she came to take notes not to talk, but then being a female, she knew when she'd been addressed, so she says, "I'm Marie Patot and this is my Uncle Boudreaux, and kind of a cousin, Pierre." I wasn't her darn cousin at all, now why would she say such a thing?

"You're down from Boston?" which was Ways home district.

"No," retorts Marie, "we all from Lafite down in Lous-e-anna." Now what's this "we all" south Mississippi act? Marie, you're a bred and buttered French Cajun, I thought, getting myself all riled up over no thin'. By this time the Congressman was sitting on the edge of his chair like a virgin on his first trip to the cat house. Uncle, the wily old devil, was not above taking advantage of an advantage, so he says, "Marie darlin', tell the Congressman what we looking for."

That Marie she have a few brains behind that smile, so she starts out, "Mr. Ways..."

He cuts in with, "My friends call me Fi, Marie."

"Fi," she says, "Uncle Boudreaux is up here representing the poor folks, who have funds in our Lafite Savings, and they want to find out what's happened to their capital?"

"Have no fear Marie, I'm one of the main stays on the financial committee investigating the malfeasance and mismanagement that has ruined our fine savings & loan industry, and burdened our taxpayers. Sorry, there's the floor call light, I must run for a quick vote. Marie, please leave your hotel with my secretary, and I'll have my limo pick you up tonight. We can talk the situation over with a steak and a glass of wine at our leisure." and he's out the door to vote.

CHAPTER 4

Marie Patot sat back relaxed in the big easy chair in her hotel room and stared at the Washington panorama presented by the view outside her window and thought, "This is what I call living."

Since Armand, her husband, had been drowned after being blown off an oil platform in the gulf four years ago, Marie had been edgy and undecided upon what to do with her life.

As a beautiful and desirable twenty-four year old widow, she had many suitors, but felt the urge to leave the bayou, for the more expansive, and exciting life, she envisioned in the city. The phone buzzed and it was Uncle Ignace. "Marie honey," he say, "what for you doin' with yourself?"

What for you doin', she thought, there had to be some refined gentlemen, that could fall in love with her. All the suitors on the bayou, were of the what for you doin' kind. "Uncle, I'm just enjoying the view of Washington."

"Marie, I get the idea, this Mr. Ways has in mind heading in your direction alone, and at this first outing, I don't think your mama going to like that. Why don't you give the Congressman a little ring and suggest, maybe your Uncle, and Pierre join you for a bite of supper?"

"Certainly, Uncle."

"Marie, let me have a call when you hear."

Marie dug out the Senator's private number, supplied by his secretary and dialed. She was surprised, when Mr. Ways himself answered the phone, "Marie Patot here."

"Why Marie, how nice to hear from you, I was just walking out the door, when the phone rang, I'm happy you caught me in time. Is anything wrong?"

"Oh no, Mr. Ways, I've just been a mite uncomfortable about our going out alone on a first date in a strange city. We Bayou girls been accustomed to knowing men fairly well before we go out alone."

Events weren't going exactly as Fi had planned, but then why not be gracious, it pays in the long run. "Why Marie, it surely would be nice to be alone with you, but that can wait, lets you and I have your Uncle and Pierre join us for dinner."

What a lovely man, thought Marie, "Fi, that's so kind of you to make the suggestion."

Marie informed Ignace of the altered dinner plans, and Boudreaux felt relieved, not knowing that a Washington politician has more moves up his sleeve, than a russian chess master.

Being a man of action and decision, Ways quickly altered his plans to meet the new development, so as to turn the situation to his advantage. In Washington, when one wanted to remove a heterosexual male obstacle from any particular scene, one merely phoned Madam Barbara, also referred to as the head of the extra-curricular secretarial pool of blondes, brunettes, redheads, all statuesque, stylish, well spoken, and expensive. Barbara came on the line as soon as she was told it was Fi calling. "Hi darling," Barbara never used names even in very intimate circumstances, it was part of her code of ethical survival, "a little something French for you tonight, or something tall, blonde, and Scandinavian?"

"Not for me Babs, I require the services of two of your stunners, to remove two Cajun bumpkins from the proximity of a flower of the Bayou, a Cajun Princess."

Barbara gave a shriek of laughter, "Why you old

fraud, are you telling me you are setting out for a legitimate try for the goods, instead of an evening‘s rental? I didn’t think you would remember the moves in that game. Besides, therein lies danger,” cautioned Babs, “Suppose you fell for her and ended up tripping up an aisle. That would be the most expensive lady you’ve ever had.”

“That isn’t it at all Babs. I just want to go out with someone I can talk to, and not know for sure how it’s going to end.”

“Ok, I’ll send Yvonne and Renee’, who shall they be, little lost elves?”

“French elves,” retorted Fi, “do they both speak French?”

“Of course darling, they’re the real sterling thing.”

“Fine, let them be lobbyists looking for American money.”

"Such high class ladies should surely demand a premium price," laughed Babs.

"But Babs, darling, I'm not a retail customer, I'll expect your usual wholesale prices."

"Wholesale it is darling, let me know as soon as the agenda is set. Keep in mind that after midnight is time and one half, and overnight is double time. My girls are members of AFL Union number 876, and we vote."

The Limo arrived at 7:30 sharp and had plenty of room for Ignace, Marie and me in the back seat. The driver took us to a place called Georgetown, up a long driveway, and under a side cupola, the place seemed familiar, and then it dawned on me, the front facade was a duplicate of the Whitehouse. I guess Congressman Ways wanted to practice up at home. In any case, after a slight toot on the horn, Mr. Ways came out, steps into the rear jump seat, and gave his driver directions to our destination.

Mr. Ways shook hands all around, and greeted Uncle and I civilly enough, but it was clear his interest centered on Marie. Something about that attention didn't appeal to me. Next thing I know, we arrive at this flambeaux lit restaurant. After a fine dinner, Mr. Ways sat back with his drink, and turned to Uncle and said, "I am really interested in the historical, and cultural background of your area of Louisiana."

This Mr. Ways was sure full of conversation designed to oil up the hearer, I thought to myself.

"But," Ways continued, "Even though I have not had the pleasure of visiting your area, as yet, I hope to go there soon. How far would you say it is from Washington?"

"Well, goin' right through trees and parked cars, it would be about a thousan' miles," estimated Uncle.

"I must make a point of getting down there, for if you have such attractive moveable scenery, (slight bow to Marie), the permanent scenery must be beautiful indeed."

Uncle and I were getting bored by this cocktail talk, so Uncle changed the subject, and addressed Ways, "Mr. Ways as I explained on the ride here, we are trying to discover what happened to the capital missing from our Lafite Savings. Without taking his eyes off Marie, Ways responded, "I don't ordinarily like to discuss business matters at dinner, however..."

Just then Ways was interrupted by the Captain, who announced the presence of two Washington lobbyists, who had sent over after dinner drinks for our table.

"Captain," says Ways, "please ask the lobbyists

if they can join us?"

Now I hear about these lobbyists in D.C., but when I see these two, it become very obvious, why lobbyists are so effective.

Ways took the taller of the two by the hand, "Gentlemen, may I present Yvonne and Renee'. These, gentlemen, are Ignace Boudreaux and Pierre LeBlanc, and Ignace's niece Marie from Lafite, Louisiana." Renee' seated her little hind side right next to me, and she start lobbying with her leg the minute she hit the chair.

Uncle Boudreaux, with that twinkle he has in his eye, turned to Ways, "I think of lobbyists as sort of fat bald men, not beautiful young ladies." Mr. Ways laughed, "Lobbyists come in all sizes shapes and genders, these days, so they can sneak up on us."

After 'bout an hours chit chat, this Yvonne

say to Uncle Boudreaux, "Mr. Boudreaux, I know a little spot out in the country, over in Virginia, where we can dance, and perhaps take a boat ride in the moonlight on the lake. It is much less crowded than this smoky old place."

"Pierre, how you feel about takin' these sports models out dancin' and honky tonkin'? Pierre, I'm talkin' to you."

I'd been so busy playing "lobby hands and knees," I just barely caught the gist of what Uncle suggested, but I remember saying, "Yea, I'm all for it, let's go."

Next thing I remember, Uncle and I, and these two French lobbyists are arriving at this little chateau inn, someplace out in the country. It occurred to me, that we had left sweet Marie in the willing hands of Mr. Ways, but knowing Marie, I decided to let Mr. Ways shift for himself.

Later I found out that Uncle was having the same lobbyist problems as me. Yvonne, hadn't started her lobbying quite as fast as Renee', but by the time Uncle has a couple of dances at the Inn, he finds himself on a nice upholstered bench by the dock, where they separate the male lobbyists from the female lobbyists.

After a half hour on the bench, Uncle decided they were well enough acquainted to proceed to more comfortable accommodations at the hotel.

Following a visit to the desk to obtain a room, Uncle and Yvonne were awaiting the descent of the elevator when the door suddenly opened, and there stood Senator Means, with an apparent sixteen year old "Lolita" on his arm.

Later at the hearings, there were several variations on the conversation that followed the encounter, but the gist was as follows:

“OH! Oh! good evening Yvonne,” sputtered Means, “allow me to introduce my niece Sally. Ah, she’s in from the country for a few days, and I’m showing her the sights.”

About this time Renee’ and I arrive at the elevator, and I hear Uncle say quietly to Yvonne, “Wonder what sights ‘Niece Sally’ might see in a country hotel bedroom? It must be true what they say, politics makes strange bed-fellow.”

Yvonne nodded agreement, “In my capacity as a lobbyist, I’ve met Means many times. He must have had many brothers and sisters, because he certainly has a large supply of young ‘nieces’ from the country, and I’ve seen this particular niece with a variety of different uncles.” This comment brought knowing chuckles and giggles from everyone. Luckily Mr. Means and his niece had proceeded into the lobby, out of range of our conversation.

Following a practically sleepless, but altogether enjoyable evening, we all had a fine breakfast, and headed on back to Washington.

After dropping off the ladies, Uncle and I proceeded back towards the hotel. Now that Uncle and I are chasing the ladies together, I venture, "Whoo boy, these gal lobbyist, sure know how to get a man's vote, or at least mine, any day. That Renee', she got a flummery eye, a honey pot tongue, plus other equipment, that make an angel turn in his wings. She got right to work on me, without a bayou leave."

I don't think Uncle was quite ready to join my young men's chasing club, because he think over what I say slowly, then comes the philosophy. "Son," he says, "we've just witnessed another classic case of 'incumbent-itis' disease at work." Damned if I could see the connection, but Uncle continued, "Congressman Ways decided he wanted to take a crack at Marie, and you and I were in the way of his plans. So he phones up one of the more exclusive stables here in Washington and arranges two 'Night Lobbyists' to entertain you and me. That was a right friendly and expensive gesture, and we both enjoyed the entertainment.

"The problem with it all, is the good Congressman has been holed up here so long in the Bingo Dome, he thinks us voters can't tell the difference between a lobbyist and a hired lady. You see son, he forget us voters from outside the Bingo Dome live, love, and think. Someday, that's goin' to prove to be a fatal mistake for the Congressman's political career."

CHAPTER 5

It took us a full day of rest and relaxation to rid ourselves of the effects of dealing with those Washington, "French Lobbyists." I done read in the paper about how everyone always lobbying the U.S. Congress. For sure, after a night with one of those lobbyists, a man about to vote for just anything she told him, just to get lobbied ag'in.

Uncle Boudreaux and I been yakkin' and throwin' some ideas around, and a thought occurred to me, "Uncle, why everyone have all those assistants running around behind them?" Uncle pumped some thoughts into his brain cell with his eyebrow, and answered, "Son, an incumbent politician in Washington, after a few years can't see past the Bingo Dome, like I tell you before. But they devised a system to solve this problem, by having all these lobbyists up here, to point the politician the way through the woods. Only one problem, when those politician move through the woods on a national scale, they make huge tracks, that are easy to follow. So the politician need all those assistant with brooms to cover the tracks, 'cause come next election, that politician may want to tell the voters he wasn't there at all."

When the afternoon paper come, it say that Mr. Charm, the Chief Regulator, was on deck ag'in for next mornin'. After last night, we need all the rest we can get, so we have a nice hotel room dinner, and hit the sack.

We get to the hearing room a little late next day, but there is Mr. Charm in the star chair all alone, and he looks like they been working him over for a few days. It's obvious, from the look on his face, he feel like an atheist at the Inquisition. Senator Means says, "Mr. Charm, why didn't your regulators crack down on these thieves?" Fella sitting next to me, turns and whispers, "This is the 21st time they ask Charm that question. I'll give five to one it makes thirty times before the day's out." Well I didn't just fall off the turnip truck, and it was obvious this fella had some inside information, so I declined.

Looking at Mr. Charm squirm, it was also obvious he was torn between telling what was on his mind, and keeping his job, so he answers, "Senator, our organization is dedicated to enforcing the rules and regulations initiated by the Congress of the United States." This put the ball in the Senators court.

It seems the Senator's time was up, so Senator Taxwriter jumps into the fray with a new question, "Mr. Charm, if your regulators had cracked down on these thieves in 1985, don't you think we could have avoided this catastrophe?" This made the twenty second time for this same question, I thought to myself.

Somehow you could see that Mr. Charm had made a decision, because for the first time a thin grin crossed his face. “Senator,” says Charm, “our records show there was no great losses in the S&L and banking industry in 1985, except those which could be attributed to the catastrophic fall in oil prices, which put certain sections of the country under great economic pressures. However, beginning in 1987 through today, there has been a continuous decline in the capital ratios of the S&L, banking, and insurance industries in the country. As you say Senator, 90% of the malfeasance and theft began after 1986. Our organization has spent a great deal of time documenting this evidence.”

This answer seemed to cause a little thought at the “judges table,” Means turns to his aid, and then to Taxwriter, and they have a little off the mike conversation. Then Taxwriter shifts his top four sheets of notes to the bottom of the stack, and says. "Mr. Charm, we are not saying your office has not performed admirably during these trying times, and I'm sure we will get to the bottom of this malfeasance and theft that has been going on. As our President says, 'We shall have them all behind bars, where they belong.' "

Not much else happened that mornin', except that fella next to me could have easily won his bet. According to my count, and I was prejudice, they asked that same question forty two times. One sort of got the opinion that someone was trying to make a point of some kind.

Heading back to the hotel in the taxi, Uncle Boudreaux didn't utter a word, then when we get out he decides, we take a turn through the park. Finally he says, "Pierre, what was said today, that had the ring of a cracked cowbell?"

This was one of the few times Uncle had asked

my advice on anything, so I was a bit taken back, and wanted to make sure I didn't sound like a new born calf. "Uncle, Mr. Charm seem to be pretty happy with his answer regarding the beginning of the thefts."

"Yes," says Uncle, "and if you watched the dais, Senator Means didn't care much for the date Mr. Charm chose for the malfeasance and theft to start.

"Pierre, me thinks we better make another trip to Charmsville, and see if Mr. Charm would like to relieve himself of some his anxieties."

Uncle made a few phone calls, and I don't know what he said. I guess he explained just how the editor of the Lafite Lagniappe had all those press privileges, 'cause when we arrive at the 12th floor, they move us directly into Mr. Charm's office and there with his hand outstretched, is Mr. Charm, greetin' us with his charmin' smile.

“Gentlemen,” gushes Mr. Charm, “I want you to know, we record all of our conversations, so we will have all of the information to follow up and adjust your grievances to your satisfaction.”

When he says this, reminds me of my cousin Joe Officer sayin’, “You have the right to an attorney, you have the right to remain silent.”

It was my understandin’, that folks like Willie Nelson were the big ones in the recordin’ business, but after a few weeks experience in Washington, I decided to call home and tell cousin Cousteau, if he plan to get in the recordin’ business, he better forget Nashville, and head on up here to D.C .

Uncle Boudreaux know this is a busy hearing man, so he gets right to the point. “Mr. Charm, we represent the depositors at the Lafite Savings, and your man say we missing $300,000. We have the same mortgage on the books, as we have five year ago, and we have a little more cash in the vault than at that time. We can't find the $300,000 your regulator say we lost. There haven't been any strangers in town lately, so we don't think there's been any thief or malfeaser like they say at the hearin'."

"Uncle," I chimed in with my new role as advisor, "we did have those two federal regulators come to town."

Mr. Charm give us his thin hearing grin, and says, "Did anyone come to see you from our office in 1985?"

"Can't say that I know for sure," answers Uncle, "but I do remember a man being in town somewhere around that time."

"No money disappeared in 85?" inquires Charm. "No," says Uncle, "if there was, no one mentioned it around town."

"Mr. Boudreaux, there was something that

could have had an effect on your little S&L during those intervening years. Congressman Ways and Senator Means authored a minor tax change in '86, which of course changed our method of evaluation of the commercial property held by your savings and loan as collateral."

"But Mr. Charm, they de same buildings now as we have den." Uncle's English really suffers, when he gets a little riled up. "You can come look see for yourself," pleads Uncle Boudreaux.

"I'm sorry Mr. Boudreaux, our office doesn't make the rules, we just follow the rules your good elected representatives make, to the best of our ability."

Charm is up, and we seem to be moving towards the door, in fact, he's helping us all the way to the elevator, and on the way, he says to Uncle, "As you can see, I'm a very busy man, but I do jog in the park at 6 a.m. each day, should you have any further questions, possibly you could join me for a little exercise." Now, wasn't that the nicest invitation Uncle and I have, since we be in this town, except of course for Yvonne and Renee'.

It is amazing the amount of joggin' talk that goes on here in Washington D.C.

CHAPTER 6

Next morning was Saturday, so uncle and I are sitting in the hotel room sort of jawin' and thinking. Finally, Uncle says, "You know boy, I keep getting the feelin' that several of those folks we been talking to, and watching, have a pretty good idea where our $300,000 done gone to, but for some reason, they don't want to share it with you and me. Now take that Cal Q. Later, he sure seemed mighty sure his ten man team could uncover that $300,000, and now Mr. Charm say something about Mr. Ways and Mr. Means changin' the rules."

"Humm," I'm thinking, "while you was talking to that fella yesterday, I was a doing some historical reading, and you know Mr. Ways and Mr. Means, their daddies were up here in Congress. In fact they named a committee after their grand-daddies. They call it the Ways and

Means Committee, the same that passed on that '86 tax law. That shore is democracy at its best, keeping those nice folks right here in the Capitol for almost hundred years."

"Son, I didn't know that fact, but I guess you could call that historical 'incumbent-itis.' "

Right about then comes a knock on the door and here's this fella we met at the country hotel the other night. "Sam I am," he announces, "just the man to solve your Lafite Savings problems."

"Come right in," Uncle and I say in unison, we were certainly looking for a solution, and Sam looked like our man. "Sam Scam," in way of reintroduction, then he takes off like a Rolls Royce engine at idle, and after appraising us of all his talents, and past achievements, along the line of finding lost S&L monies, he revved it up into high gear and says, "Gentlemen, experienced men of the world like yourselves, know that nothing is free, however, I will be representing you on a completely fair and honest basis. I will expect no funds until your problem is solved."

This sounded reasonable to me. "However," Sam continued, "the introducer in New York City, is a highly reputable attorney, and we will need to place him on retainer."

I had a bull on a retainer once, but Uncle Boudreaux, he seem to get the picture, and a little frown cross his nose. Sam, he see the frown and say, "Of course my fee is 10 % upon delivery, but I intend to come up with my portion of the retainer up front. Sam invests right along with his partners." Sam estimated $5,000 should get the entire situation moving.

We talk this over, and it seems we are to see Mr. I. B. Deeppockets the following day, Sunday, in New York City. Uncle Ignace agrees to our part of the retainer, but he no fool, he don't pay 'till we walk into the Deeppocket's door.

We pack the overnight bag, and off we go to New York, on the flyer train.

While Uncle is findin' the mens' room in that Grand Central Station, I'm a gazing and looking at that high ceiling, when I feel a slight touch and this fella say, "See this ring, a ten carat beauty, I need some quick money, so I'll let you have it for a quick $5,000."

Didn't want this city fella to think us Bayou folks weren't worldly enough to know, that a ten carat diamon' was worth more than $5,000, so I say, "Where you get this stone?"

"Lucky," he says, "just found it in the mens' room."

So, I look it over kinda expert like, and say, "Nice lookin' ring, but I don't have $5,000 cash on me right now."

"Look," he say, "I really need the money, I'll take $500 cash for a quick sale."

There come Uncle Boudreaux, so I say, "No, can't handle it today," and start off towards Uncle.

But this fella is right on my tail, sayin', "Last offer, fifty bucks." Now I don't want Uncle involved in this, so I figure I'll rid of this guy once and for all. "Five bucks," says I, "Sold," says he, so now I'm the proud owner of a ten carat $5,000 diamon' ring.

We come to this 54th Street building just like Sam says, and there is Sam waiting for us. In we go and up to the 49th floor, and it seems that Sam has lost his key, but the janitor is there and lets us in. We sit down, and in a couple of minutes in comes this silver grey haired man, who turns out to be none other than I. B. Deeppockets, himself. Sam introduces us, and pulls out his $500, and Uncle gives his $4500 to our partner, who heads cross town to give the retainer to the Attorney.

"I normally don't come down to the office on Sunday," volunteers I. B., "but my attorney insisted. So tell me your problem, I'm sure we can handle it."

Uncle relates the entire story to I. B. and ends up with the missing $300,000 capital. Mr. I. B. is taking a few notes as we go along, and he say, when uncle finish, "It seems that your strip shopping center is at the center of your problem. Tell you what I'd be willing to recommend to the board. You tell the owner of that shopping center, we'd be willing to give him $500,000 cash."

I could see, that Uncle did not cotton to this solution at all, but he remain calm and cool. "$500,000," say Uncle Boudreaux, "the center cost, $1,000,000, and Lafite Savings have $800,000 loan on the center."

"Mr. Boudreaux," retorts I. B., "I fully understand your position, but keep in mind if you jump on this offer right away, you'll save your friends $250,000."

Now this high finance is movin' awful fast for a couple of bayou traders, but we been a trading all our lives, and this goin' take a lot of explaining. "Mr. Deeppockets," say Uncle, "you wouldn't mind explainin' this savin' in a bit more detail?"

"Certainly, certainly," says I. B. "Let's start with the simple facts. The owner of the center put up $200,000 and borrowed $800,000 from Lafite Savings, correct?"

"Correct," say Uncle Boudreaux. "Now based on the tax rules in '85," continues I. B., "the owner was getting a 10% after tax return on his money. Now in 1986 Representative Ways and Senator Means passed a law that changed the tax rules. Under the new rules a new buyer can only invest $700,000, and still get a 10% after tax return.

I did some quick numbers and $1,000,000 less $700,000 was our $300,000.

"Now," says I. B., "have you ever seen an icy stand at the State Fair on a hot summer day?"

I popped in to answer, "Yes, I've stood in those hot lines and had to pay $1.50 for one small icy."

"That's right," says I. B., "and if they have any left-over next winter, you can buy the same icy for ten cents. Do you know why?" queries I. B., and he answers his own question, "because there are no buyers for icys in the winter. Gentlemen that is free enterprise at its best."

"That may make good icy sense," says Uncle Boudreaux," but I still haven't saved $250,000 on the shopping center."

"Friend," says I. B., "the same tax law of '86, that reduced the value of your center to $700,000, also eliminated your potential buyers, as sure as winter weather eliminated the icy buyers. No buyers, lower prices, so now we're down to my 'no buyers' price of $500,000. Certainly a fine honest offer, if I've ever made one."

You could see from the pain in Uncle's face, that he still didn't see no $250,000 saving. "I know what you're thinking," I. B. continued, "Where is the $250,000 saving? Keep in mind friend Boudreaux, my offer is only good now, but in a short time, the regulators are going to take over your little S&L, and when they do, they'll have a fire sale. Now we all been to the fire sale and know prices are slashed, right?"

That was the way most fire sales worked, I thought. Going right on after seeing Uncle nod his head, I. B. says, "Fire sale price going to be

$250,000. My price today, $500,000 minus the fire sale price of $250,000 equals your $250,000 saving. Your good friend I. B. Deeppockets just saved your friends $250,000. That sure ought to be worth something, don't you think?"

I'd been taking a few notes, and when I looked over the numbers, it did seem that we'd saved $250,000. On second thought, the shopping center was still there, with the same tenants, same land, same buildings, and same rents being paid. Looked to me like we now had $750,000 that had disappeared.

Kinda looked like if we waited until the selling stampede was over, and the way they keep changing those laws in Washington, sooner or later, they'd change the law back to where it was, and then like magic, that 'ole shopping center be worth $1,000,000 again, and 'ole I. B. Deeppockets goin' to have a $750,000 profit at the expense of us folks in Lafite.

"Gentlemen, now that the explanations are all out of the way, we need to get things moving towards a sale, so you can get your $250,000 saving right away," explains I. B.

"I'm in a position to start today with the financial arrangements, however, we will need to place the sales escrow deposit with the closing attorney as soon as possible. To insure good faith on both sides, normally the escrow deposit is split 50-50 between buyer and seller. Ten per cent of the price is the normal escrow deposit. As the buyer's representative, I will place his $25,000 with the escrow attorney, and you can have your $25,000 in my hands by Monday. Then we'll begin drawing up the legal documents."

"Our mutual friend Sam, will stay close to you, and you can give him the funds. Sam is a fine honest man. Been doing business with Sam for at least twenty years, never once has he defaulted on a pledge of any kind."

Thus far Sam certainly had performed as advertised, said he'd introduce us to a man who could solve our problem, and he produced the man, I. B. Deeppockets.

"There is no question in my mind, that I am dealing with the same high caliber honest type men as Sam Scam, so if you will excuse me, I have another meeting," and out the door goes I. B.

Saw I. B. slip the janitor fifty dollars for holdin' the door for him. That I. B. must have been some rich to tip like that.

We left standing there with the Janitor holding the door, anxious to lock her up. Uncle comes from that 1930s depression generation, who aren't that big on tipping, so I slip the janitor a five spot on the way out.

Looks like nothin' left to do, but head back to the Capitol.

We sitting on that fast train, watchin' the scenery go by, and I'm trying to make head or tails of this capital disappearance situation. It kinda hard for a young man to understand what happenin'. I remember the first time Uncle take me to Washington, when I was just a young feller. Seems Father Donavon had got wind of a program, they call the #236 program, for the building of apartments for the poor folks, and he get Uncle Boudreaux to head on up to Washington to see how Lafite going to get their share of the loot.

Uncle hadn't been rovin' and reportin' very long at that time. In any case, we pulls up in front of this big building and head in through the main hall. This was the first time I see all those draft carriers scurryin' about. This Senator Downtrodden was the man who sponsored the

#236. What with Uncle's press card, we didn't have much trouble getting a private interview with Senator Downtrodden. The lady up front showed us right into this big office, along with no more than hundred other private interviewers.

"Well," said Senator Downtrodden, "we are never too busy to give our individual attention to the citizens of our great country."

Then he made a few remarks about his contributions to our great country. I had no idea one man could do so much for us citizens, but the Senator thought of more things in the next fifteen minutes, than I could have imagined in a lifetime.

Senator Downtrodden looked like he be here a few years before I was born, and just before the question part began, I hear his secretary whisper that he couldn't go to his private island this weekend, because Senator Travels and some lady friends were using the place to hold a meeting on the vanishing species of the South Atlantic Live Mouth Fish. I don't think Senator Downtrodden was pleased, but then it's hard for a young fellow to discern the feeling of wise old men of wisdom, like Senator Downtrodden.

Come question time, Uncle Boudreaux is first one out of the box, he say, "Senator, the poor folks down Lafite way certainly appreciate your efforts with your #236 housing program, but in looking it over, it say right there on page one, that there is only goin' to be $600 million dollars. The Washington Post, he say the same thing. Now, Senator, when you spread that big bunch of monies all around the entire U.S. of A, it don't leave much for Lafite."

"You're quite right," .. says the Senator, then he turns, and on the side, says to his aid, "any press here today?" I didn't catch the reply, but it seems there was not, of course Uncle bad not mentioned being the roving reporter for the Lafite Lagniappe, but maybe that don't count.

In any case the Senator continues, "Of course, young man, you understand our legislation extends for 30 years?"

"You in the back row," calls the Senator.

Uncle Boudreaux grab my hand, and we took off for the other side of the room, like a gator after a pigeon. Uncle's hat went on, and on goes his coat, and his hand went up, and was a shaken faster than a fat ladies chops on a bull ride.

"Fellow with the hat," says the Senator, "do you have a question?"

Well I never knew this was my Uncle Boudreaux talkin', he up and says, "I say ole chap, $600 million for 30 years, isn't that eighteen billion dollars? Don't you think with the new Full Disclosure Law the total amount should have been reported to the press, and disclosed on the front page of your legislation, and included in the next 30 years budget?"

Uncle he one fine newspaper man. First he find out where that money goin', now he put on his other hat and ask, who goin' pay all that money?

"The cost has been well publicized, and believe me, housing is a dire need of our country," replied the Senator.

On the way home from that Washington trip, the words of my Uncle Joe came to me loud and clear. He was telling Mr. Bill at the feed store, that Phil Sleezy, his competitor, was advertising his houses for $4,000 and getting all the customers. Uncle Joe said, that after Phil signed them all up, the customers found out they owed Phil Sleezy $4,000 per year for 30 years. The net result was they got after Phil, and sent him to Leavenworth, seems he violated the Truth in Lending and Truth in Advertising Laws. I've often wondered since, if they passed a Truth in Legislation Law?

When we were home a while, Father Donavon said, they sent two government teams into Lafite to set up the number 236 program. One figured out what our poor folks could afford to pay, and the other calculated what the cost of the housing was going to be. Father Donavon said, those experts were correct to the penny in both cases.

There was one hitch though, it seems that the amount the poor folks could pay, plus the government grant available, wasn't enough to pay for the notes on the housing. Seems these team experts forgot to talk to each other.

One thing for sure, Lafite didn't get our share of that eighteen billion dollars, 'cause we don't have none of those number 236 housing. I did hear they build a whopping big bunch of them number 236s up there where they vote for Senator Downtrodden.

CHAPTER 7

Next day, I reminded Uncle Boudreaux, about all those number 236 our folks paid taxes for, and the fact we didn't get a single one in Lafite. He and I chat a while and we decide, that we been skinned once by these folks in Washington, and we weren't about to let the same thing happen again.

"Pierre," says Uncle, "adding up what Charm, Cal Q. and Deeppockets has tole us, it seems we started out on the right track with Congressman Ways, but we really need the help of Senator Byall Means, if we goin' to get these problem turned around. Now, we met Senator Means the other night, while we was cavortin' with those ladies, and I got a feeling he might just listen to what an ole Cajun has to say."

So me, and the ole Cajun hi-tailed it over to the Senate office building to find Senator Means.

We find his office, which turn out to be a whole passel of offices, but one bv one we get bv the secretarial and assistant guard with Uncle Boudreaux 's press card, until we hit the final challenge, Miss Hassel. It looked like there was no way we goin' to get past Miss Hassel, to the Senator, until Uncle sidles up to her and says, "Please tell the Senator that I'm the fellow, who met the Senator, and his young - niece at the Country Inn over in Virginia last week."

Miss Hassel couldn't hold it back, and ex-claimed, "That Two Timing Rat." Now I never hear such language from a saucy little secretary like Miss Hassel, but she get red in the face and say, "Of course, I'll personally take you right in, follow me."

In we go, Senator Means is talking on the telephone, but that don' deter Miss Hassel, she announces, "Senator you have some very, very, important visitors. Some of your close friends from the Chateau Inn. Sit right here," indicating the chairs at his desk, "the Senator will be more than delighted to talk with you the minute he gets off the phone."

The Senator looks at Miss Hassel, then at Uncle and me, and says, "Charlie, let me call you right back." He hang up the phone, stares at Uncle and blurts, "What do you want," in a not too friendly manner.

Now this don't bother Uncle one iota. Uncle smiles, looks graciously at the Senator and says, "Senator, as one ole reprobate to another, I shore could use some good down to earth advice."

This didn't sound too threatening to the Senator, so he says, "I'm a very busy man Mr.," and Uncle supplies the name, "Ignace Boudreaux from Lafite Louisiana, and my nephew, Pierre."

Uncle continues, "No sir, we won't take much of your time, just a little advice, and we on our way." The Senator says, "I'm rather short of advice at this time, but tell me what you have in mind?"

Now Uncle relates the entire story to Senator Means, about the regulators comin' to Lafite, about our discussions with Mr. Cal Q., and Mr. Charm, and even about our offer from Mr. Deeppockets. The Senator seemed to have lost interest in the short time he had available, for it took Uncle a good hour to relate the entire story.

You could see Senator Means mellowing, as the story continued, and when Uncle finished, the Senator smiled for the first time and said, "Ignace, you have certainly come to the right man for advice. It's obvious to me that you have been picking up bits and pieces of information, but no one has filled you in on the big picture. Your's is obviously the exception to the rule. We have been faced in this country with some terrible cases of fraud, mismanagement, and downright stealing. If it weren't for the backing of the SLIC by your federal government here in Washington, many of the small depositors throughout the entire country would have been wiped out. But laws, I personally shepherded through Congress, saved the day. Let me look into your situation. You just head on back to Lafite, and don't give this problem another thought. Believe me, from what you tell me, the regulators have made an error in your case, and I am absolutely sure it will be corrected. Mr. Deeppocket's story is pure fantasy."

Uncle sure hit the target with Senator Means. He was obviously, one of the finest, and most powerful men in the Country, and he had just told Uncle Boudreaux the problem was solved. I was ready to head on home to Lafite. In any case, there wasn't much more to say to Senator Means, except thank you, which we did, and as we were walking out of the office, I heard the buzzer ring at Miss Hassel's desk.

Some of the things I'm going to relate to you, Uncle Boudreaux, and I didn't know about at the time, but you know how the Washington hearing has now replace the ole "soap opera" on TV, so when the cow dung start to blow into the fan, they had a pot full of hearin', to find out who was covering up what, and I mean the Bingo balls were bouncing around the inside of that Washington dome like the shootin' stars in Star Wars II. One of the main atheist, to be before the tribunal, was ole Senator Byall Means, so we heard a lot of detail on his doings, and everyone else we met, while we were in Washington.

After we left the office, ole Byall flicked on his recordin' system and headed for the office door. Opening the door he calls, "Miss Hassel!"

Miss Hassel, Byall's number one assistant,

attaches her micro recorder to her note pad, and heads for Byall's office. As she passes by he gives her little bottom a few friendly pats, since friendly pats are not recordable, and she flashes him her "You Rat," who were you with last week, look. They have the usual recorder talk about the day's events, during which, Means finds out that Representative Bulgebottom's district contains Lafite, Louisiana. Knowing he is in the dog house, Byall suggests that Miss Hassel take the rest of the day off. When she left, Byall picked up the phone, and dialed Bulgebottom's private line. "Senator Means here, to speak with my good friend Congressman Bulgebottom."

Now Bulgebottom hadn't heard from Senator Means in twenty years, so he was on the phone pronto, right now. "Bulgebottom, my good friend," says Means, "I was planning to do my daily aerobics in the senate garage, and thought we might breathe together in about ten minutes."

With this statement, Senator Means being a man of very few words on such occasions, hung the phone up.

Only in Washington do grown men do their garage aerobics in a suit and tie, but there they were, Senator Means and Congressman Bulgebottom, prepared for heavy breathing. "Bulgebottom," says to Means, in a not too friendly voice, "who the hell is this Cajun from your district, been running all around town, and up to New York City, asking questions about his Lafite Savings, and the capital they lost?"

Bulgebottom had to give this some thinkin', 'cause he didn't remember any Cajun. Then out of the blue came the name Lafite. Of course Lafite was in his district, in fact the entire Bulgebottom family was from Lafite. Come to think of it, he was from Lafite himself. "Why Senator, I put that Boteau, no, Boudreaux on the plane myself personally, just a few weeks ago. Did he come back?"

"Come back," screeched Means, "that Cajun never left!"

After reading the riot act to Bulgebottom, and sending him on his way, to have two Cajuns expelled from Washington by the following morning, if not sooner, Senator Means returned to his office to make one more call.

"Hi Fi, By, here," chortles Senator Means. "Why you old scoundrel," says Ways, "looking for a golf game, or an afternoon at Bab's Senate Caucus room?"

"Findmore, we need to take a ride to the country to look over the farm," comes back Means.

"Farm? What farm, you buy a farm over in Virginia By?"

Damn, thought Means, if it wasn't for his grand-daddy, that boy would be selling pencils in Boston. "You'll love the farm," says Means, "I'll pick you up in twenty minutes."

Once Findmore and Byall are out in the open country, where only the Lord and Byall records conversations, Byall begins, "Findmore, remember how we sponsored the 'Ways & Means' tax bill back in '86?"

"Sure," says Ways, "you said we need that fifteen billion increase in taxes to get the administration to go along on the budget package."

"That's right," says Byall, "but in hindsight, it seems we made a small miscalculation. Instead of raising fifteen billion, like we planned, it seems we are going to lose over 500 billion."

"What!" Findmore is taken back, he doesn't know anything about any Five Hundred Billion

Dollars.

“It’s a serious situation,” agrees Byall, “but with a little insight into the world of the Press, the situation can be handled. You see, Findmore, to be successful in dealing with anyone, the first step is to understand their motives. Now in the case of the Press, we have a capitalistic enterprise, whose prime objective is the selling of advertising. The greater the audience the greater the monies from the advertising.”

Continuing his educational discourse, Byall says, “The voters understand small things, such as two thousand dollar toilet seats, thousand dollar trips to New York, and they love scandal of any kind. When it comes to the big ticket items, up in the billions, the news loses reality to the average voter.

The net result is, it is much easier to cover up a large disaster than a small indiscretion. Keeping the press happy is similar to keeping your pet dog happy, you just keep feeding them small bones one at a time for each day's headline." Byall explains, "Up to now I've had the entire situation under control, but something has happened, and I may need your help to keep this thing under wraps."

"I don't understand, Byall, if I'm going to be of any help, you've got to fill me in on all the details. Don't misunderstand, I'm with you all the way, just like always."

"I'm sure I can count on you Fi," says Byall. Byall begins his explanation, "As you recall the taxes were all to be paid by the other party's voters, so it didn't cost us a single vote. But I didn't count on the capitalist system with all its ramifications. You see, when we changed the tax rules on real estate to pick up our extra fifteen billion, all those real estate buyers changed the prices they were willing to pay for the stuff. It seems they wanted the same after tax rate of return on their money, as before we made the tax changes. The net result was a decrease of the appraised value of every piece of commercial real estate in the country. It took a while, but when they started to sell what the S&L's and banks had mortgages on, they found out that there wasn't enough value left to pay off the mortgages. We sent the regulators in, and they confirmed the values.

"So now we have the S&L' s going under, the banks getting ready to go under, and the insurance companies wavering."

"My god," exclaimed Findmore, "this is a national catastrophe!"

"Findmore," says Ways very seriously, "this can be much worse than that, we could get thrown out of office."

"Now up until four weeks ago, I had the

situation damage control in good order," explains Means. "We put up the usual smoke screen, with all the disinformation. We can thank the Ruskies for that lesson. Found a patsy, who was running a bad show right from the start, had all those nationally televised hearings, the news media loved it. Even conned the President into making that statement about putting all those crooks in jail. When that calmed down, we had hearings on the regulators and how inept they all were, and finally, we put five of our very own up as sacrificial lambs. Then the Arab war came along, and took over the front page, and it looked like we were home free.

"Now, out of nowhere, comes this Cajun wanting to know what happened to their capital at the Lafite Savings.

"The problem with their Lafite Savings situation is there isn't any thief, and the reason for their failure is so obviously our tax law, that if some smart newsman, who could add and subtract, should get wind of this, he'd blow the entire smoke screen out of the water."

Findmore was taking all of this in, and it looked like a complicated mess to him. "What can I do to help?" hoping Means hadn't found out about his relationship with Marie. He had planned to keep the uncle on the string with his Lafite Savings problem, as an extra hook into Marie. Now the entire situation had changed from a little lady chasing, to controlling a political disaster. After thinking his position over, he decided for sure, that now was not the time to broach the subject with Means.

The two men drove back to the Capital, each contemplating what his next move should be. Then Means decided belatedly to answer Findmore' s question, "Come to think of it, I may not need your help, I think I've found a way to put this situation to bed, once and for all."

CHAPTER 8

Being a member of the press corps, Uncle Boudreaux liked to frequent the bars where the members of the 4th estate congregated. One evening Uncle spots this fellow in a tweed jacket.

So Uncle says, "look there is my old drinking buddy Tom English." Uncle reels in Tom and the first thing you know, we been having quite a few, and the conversation turns from females to business.

It seems that Tom is now the financial editor for the London Times, and he's over here covering some kind of money changin' convention between the various finance ministers.

Now Uncle realizes that his friend should be an expert on capital disappearance problems, so Uncle explains the Lafite Savings problem to Tom English in great detail. It seems that Tom takes a real interest in our problem. Gets out his little pad, and starts jotting down notes as Uncle unfolds our trials and travels here in Washington and New York.

Just about the time Tom gets ready to start explaining what he thinks happened to our capital at Lafite Savings, Marie comes a rushin' in all excited. It seems that Representative Bulgebottom has been calling frequently, and it looks like he done solved our problem completely.

So we assure Tom that we'll all meet right smart soon, and off we go to the hotel, to contact Senator Bulgebottom.

When we get to the hotel, there's ole Bulgebottom, and about four of his assistants sittin' right there in the lobby, 38-24-36 was missing. Talk about service, when us constituents goes to Washington, this was certainly beyond all expectations.

When we first arrive Congressman Bulgebottom look mighty unhappy, but when he see Uncle Boudreaux, Marie and me, his face light up like he just saw the Madonna in a vision. "My friend Boudreaux, we've been looking all over town for you."

"Ignace," it seems we are now on first name terms, "your Lafite Capital problem has been solved. We have taken the liberty of packing your luggage, which is right here in the lobby, and my limousine is standing by, to whisk you, and your party, directly to the airport."

"That's mighty neighborly of you," says Uncle, "but we don't have no reservation on a plane."

"Nonsense, Ignace, the Tokyo Industries jet is headed right in the direction of Lafite, and I have arranged for them to give you a free lift." Senator Bulgebottom has turned into one of the most accommodating folks, I have ever met.

No question about it, being a member of the Press Corps really makes a difference in this man's world.

Uncle Boudreaux says, "Well Bulge, you wouldn't mind passing on to me just what this solution would be?" I could see Uncles line of reasoning. We had a couple other solutions, to this capital problem, that weren't exactly what we had in mind as a solution.

"Details, details," says Bulgebottom, "Details are what you elect your Washington representative for. We'll wrap up those details, and package them like they was a Neiman's Christmas gift." All the while, Bulgebottom has Uncle by the arm, and we seem to be moving towards the revolving door exit to the lobby.

Uncle pulls to a halt, and says, "We haven't paid the hotel bill."

"All taken care of, says Bulgebottom, "They're forwarding it to Lafite Savings direct."

"Bulge," says Uncle, and I could see he was getting a bit riled by Representative Bulgebottoms actions, "you know I'm a man of honor, and no honorable Bayou man is goin' to stand up a meeting with a good frien'."

"Who might your good friend be?" solicits Bulge.

"Tom English is his name, I doubt you would know him. If you don't mind, I think we'uns just stay over until tomorrow, so's my friend and I can share a little bread and wine over lunch. Then with all my obligations out of the way, we hop right on that plane for Lafite."

You could see Bulgebottom thinking this over, and of course at the time, I didn't know about his conversation with Senator Means, but I guess

Bulgebottom felt this would save him an extra free jet ride. He could use it himself for his next Caribbean jaunt. On this issue, one more day certainly couldn't make a difference, so why not indulge Boudreaux's whim.

"Ignace, if that's the way you want to do it, we certainly are here to serve your wants. My limo, will pick you up here tomorrow afternoon at 3 p.m. sharp."

With this little piece of business out of the way, Bulgebottom hustled back to the office where to his dismay, a Mr. Joe Follower, from Senator Mean's staff was waiting. Joe Follower was not a man to be put off, and he moves right in on Representative Bulgebottom, and in his most polite manner, which was on the order of a shovel being pushed across dry concrete, Follower says, "Congressman, the Senator asked me to check with you on the whereabouts of a few of your Cajun constituents, and pass the word to him at the club."

"Tell my good friend Byall, those folks are as good as on the plane to Lafite," replies Bulgebottom. Now Follower can read Washingtonian English really well, so he says, "Are they on the plane, in the air, headed in the direction of Lafite this minute?"

"Not exactly," says Bulgebottom, "but they are lined up to leave promptly at 3 p.m. tomorrow."

"It's very nice of you to pass this information on to me, Congressman, hope you have a nice day." and Follower departed. Bulgebottom was not in his office over ten minutes, 'till the private line rings, and it's none other than Senator Means, himself.

"Bulgebottom! What's this I hear about tomorrow being the Cajun travel date?"

"Now, Senator," says Bulgebottom, "we didn't

want to seem to make the exit too apparently urgent, and besides, Boudreaux had a luncheon engagement with an old friend from the U.K tomorrow."

Means smelled something he didn't like, "What's this friend's name?"

"Think his name was something English," was the reply.

"Tom English!" exclaims Means. "Yes, I believe that's the name."

Oh Lord, thought Means, some day I'm going to leave this place. No sense explaining who Tom English was to this idiot Bulgebottom. If you're going to get something important done, you do it yourself, especially in this city. "See that your man does not miss tomorrows flight," and Bulgebottom's reply was to a dial tone.

If Tom English gets wind of this cover up all

hell is going to break loose. English had a mind that worked 38 hours per day and understood numbers like an IBM 7020. Byall gave this new development some serious thought. The entire situation was fast getting out of hand.

Dialing a New York City number, Byall said, “Dollar, Byall here.” Dollar Banks was one of the foremost members of the American financial community. “Dollar,” says Means, “I have come across one of the nicest little shopping center investments you have ever seen. I’ll bet one of your borrowers would be delighted to have an opportunity to scoop this up.”

“Of course Byall, always keeping an eye out for the welfare of our borrowing customers. How many million will it take?”

“One,” says Byall.

“One! You know Byall that type of small deal

is for the locals, we normally don't get involved in these small loans."

"Have your man contact Jacque Shopper in Lafite, Louisiana," says Means, then he continues, "This is a firm million dollar price, one of the best buys your customer will ever make, and a stellar loan for your bank. One jewel of a strip center," offers Byall as an afterthought.

Now Dollar can't imagine, why Means would be so interested in a dinky little shopping center in the middle of nowhere. On the other hand, the new banking regulations are coming up, and Byall Means is Chairman of the Senate Banking Committee. "How fast do you think our customer will need to move in order not to miss this opportunity?" queries Dollar.

"I'd say, if he arrived this afternoon with a cashier's check, he might be able to close tonight, or early tomorrow morning." was Means reply.

"Done, Byall," says Dollar.

"Always a pleasure to help out a friend," says Means, and the conversation ends.

One last move thinks Byall, if only I could figure a way to bi-pass that Bulgebottom. Satisfied with the progress of his plan, and seeing the end to the dilemma, Byall allows himself a little chuckle, picturing the Congressman's fat rear end in a chair, he certainly was aptly named. "Congressman," says Means, "please have your Cajun friend call home early tomorrow morning, I'm sure they have found that capital the Lafite Savings lost. So he can head right on back to Lafite."

Bulgebottom was no fool about the important things, and he was a figurin', there was somethin' here he could get a lot of browny points from, if he could just get an inkling of the nature of the problem. Byall Means was not a man to get so excited about a happening in Lafite. Bulgebottom was to ponder that question, until they had those hearings with Senator Byall Means as the chief witness, and even then, he really never understood what happened.

Uncle hadn't really planned to see his friend Tom English again, but it was a good excuse to buy some time, and figure out what was happenin', and when all of these solutions were about to come about, if ever. It's nice to be assured that your problems are all solved, but it's even nicer to have the cash in the bank.

Along about 11:30 a.m. Uncle gets a call from Lafite, and it's Father Donovan.

"Ignace," says the good Father, "you will never believe this, but Jacque Shopper walked into the Lafite Saving this mornin', and laid down $800,000 to pay off his loan. It looks like we have lots more cash in the vault, but it really does cut into our income to lose our biggest and best loan. I don't know where we goin' to find any really good loans, like the one on the shoppin' center?"

Uncle Boudreaux, couldn't answer that question, but it seems that all of these good folks up here in Washington were 100% correct, for the capital problem had been taken care of, even if the capital disappearance mystery had not been solved.

That afternoon, right on time, the Congressmen's limousine picked us up, and we were all off to Lafite.

CHAPTER 9

Now we're all back in Lafite, mindin' our own business, with the Lafite Savings in fine shape with the regulators. Those regulators showed up the very next day, after that loan was paid off, and gave the Lafite Savings a clean bill of health.

The Lafite Savings held a meeting for all the folks who had their savings at Lafite, and Uncle Boudreaux told them the good news how we managed to recover all the lost capital. Then he explained the bad news for everyone in the district, 'cause when you take that 500 billion dollars the Ways and Means tax law going to cost, and divide it by the number of Congressional districts in the U.S., our district's share come to over one billion dollars in increased taxes. At this point Joe Broussard our local CPA asked, "Why didn't our Congressman Bulgebottom blow the whistle on this error before it got underway?"

Uncle replies, “I can’t speak for the Congressman, but in general a billion dollars here, a billion dollars there, don’t mean much to those folks in Washington, what with them counting so many of those billions, I guess he just didn’t have time to get involved.”

“May not mean much to Bulgebottom, but I figure my share to be right at $15,000, and that’s lots of money to me and to lots of other folks in this room,” replied Joe Broussard.

And I thought, a 38-24-36 can take a lot of a man’s time, but then a billion dollars in increased taxes to the district shouldn’t be too much to keep a fine man like Congressman Bulgebottom in Washington.

Looks like I was wrong, cause later on down at the feed store, I heard them talkin’, and they didn’t think they were willing to pay a billion dollars to keep Congressman Bulgebottom in Washington.

One fella said, "We been putting those attorneys up in Washington, 'cause we figured they were dealin' in laws, but it looks like they really dealin' in our money. Seems like we need to send someone like Joe Broussard, the CPA, up there, at least we know he can count."

Turns out that wily ole Uncle of mine knew where that capital had disappeared all along. For those of you who like numbers, I've included some of Uncle's financial notes on the strip center in the Epitaph of this little narrative.

When I ask Uncle about those numbers, he say, "Son, those politicians weren't about to admit they made a mistake. So you and I go to Washington, apply a little pressure here and there, and guess what, out of nowhere come a man with a million dollars to solve our problem."

Uncle chuckles, "Those Washington folks are so easy with other folk's money. What with the new

Ways and Means tax law, that New York fella put up $200,000, and borrow $800,000, and he have a fine return on his investment of minus 3.2%."

"That's mighty fine for us Uncle," I replied, "but what about all those other folks who didn't go to Washington? Where they goin' to find folks that are looking for a minus 3.2% return on their investments?"

"We just might have done them and the rest of the constituents in our district a mite of good also," says Uncle, "have you read the mornin' London Times?" So, I pick up the London Times and the headline on Times financial page read:

WASHINGTON RAISES 15 BILLION IN TAXES BY DECREASING THE APPRAISED VALUE OF COMMERCIAL REAL ESTATE IN USA BY TWO TRILLION DOLLARS.

You know how the English like to poke fun at

the Americans, so then it go on to say it only cost the American taxpayers 500 billion dollars to raise the 15 billion. Had a lot more to say about how the English should hustle over to the States, and pick up the bargains that the taxpayers had subsidized.

Uncle Boudreaux's friend, Tom English, wrote the article. I guess most of you didn't see the article, not many folks read the London Times as avidly as we Cajuns do.

EPITAPH

WASHINGTON D. C.

Here lies our own Congressional Ways and Means Committee, died, dead, from self inflicted foot wounds, received in 1986.

Uncle Boudreaux's Notes:

THE 500 BILLION DOLLAR "SNOWBALL"

The financial crisis began in the late 1970's with inflation at 15-17% and interest rates from 16-20%. Government actions are the primary cause of inflation in any country.

Financial Institutions who had lent money long term at 6-8% were paying 14-16% for savings, which gave them a negative cash flow of 8% on their total assets. No lender can sustain this situation for an extended length of time.

In the early 1980's government had a choice of sending in the Regulators to appraise all assets at "Market Value," or buying time by changing the investment rules and bringing inflation and interest rates back in line. Had government appraised at "Market Value," institutions holding large volumes of long term federal and municipal paper would have been "Bankrupt." At this time 30 year U. S. Government Treasury Bonds, purchased 10 years prior to date of valuation, were valued at less than 80% of their purchase price.

Happily, government chose not to create a financial crisis. Rather, they went to work lowering inflation and interest rates and passed laws liberalizing the investments of S&L' s.

SNOWBALL, Step I:

In 1986 the House of Representatives, who are the only branch of government that can initiate taxation, reported out tax legislation which extended depreciation on real estate and eliminated the expensing of real estate and many other business investment losses against ordinary earned income. This law was designed to raise additional tax revenue. Ultimately the law will cost the taxpayers in excess of 500 billion dollars.

Had Washington talked to any real estate investor, they could have learned that all investments sell on "after tax rate of return." Consequently, the 1986 tax law "devalued every piece of commercial real estate in the USA." This was a paper loss until the property was sold or appraised. Had the assets of banks and S&L's been appraised at market value the day after the law passed most would have been "Bankrupt."

SNOWBALL, Step II:

Unlike the early eighties, after creating the potential financial disaster, government sent in the regulators to appraise all assets held at "Market Value." The regulators obliged by confirming the devaluation of property legislated by Congress.

SNOWBALL, Step III:

Rather than attempting to solve 97% of the problem, which was the results of their 1986 tax law, Congress directed all of its hearing and press power at 3% of the problem, which was mismanagement by S&L's of the early 1980's liberalization program, and supposed misadministration by the Regulators, who in fact were just trying to regulate an impossible situation created by Congress. Once chastised at the Congressional Hearings, the Regulators began enforcement with a vengeance, which they are continuing to this date.

SNOWBALL, Step IV:

While on the surface continuous appraisal of a financial institutions assets based on "Today's Market Value," would seem prudent, in the long run it will eliminate the investment by financial institutions in any long term fixed rate paper including U.S. government, City, and State bonds, since the financial institutions cannot afford to risk interest fluctuations, which would lower the asset value, and consequently subject the institution to takeover by the Federal Government. All long term investments will be limited to variable rate interest paper.

SNOWBALL, Step V:

After their "Market Value" appraisals of the Congressional handiwork, the next step was the takeover of a large portion of the S&L assets in the USA. In the New Orleans area the takeover represented in excess of 70% of total assets.

Savings & Loans and Banks are not qualified to manage commercial property, and it is very doubtful if the U.S. Government is qualified to manage any commercial venture. Thus we now have properties valued by the market place at $1,000,000 prior to the 1986 tax law, being sold by the Resolution Trust Corporation for $250,000. We all know who is picking up the $750,000 in devaluation.

SNOWBALL, Step VI:

The "SNOWBALL" cost to date is estimated at 500 Billion Dollars, money you, your children, and grandchildren will be paying, since as presently constituted Congress will just keep borrowing the money and taxing you for the interest.

With a little "HOMEWORK" the initial objectives could have been met at no cost to the general taxpayer. In recent years the Congress of the United States has decided to Micro-Manage both foreign and domestic policy. One man could not read in a lifetime all of the documents proposed in Congress in just one year. The Soviet Union tried Micro-Management from the top and failed.

This 500 Billion Dollar tax error was the direct result of Congress trying to manage everything from the size of toilet seats in our bathrooms to the foreign intrigue in every third world country on the planet. There is not enough time in the year for one body of men to undertake this task efficiently.

The subsequent **COVER-UP** of their error is just business as usual.

The numbers in Uncle Boudreaux's notes on the strip center demonstrate the devaluation effects of the 1986 tax law on a commercial property. In this example everything was held constant except taxes. The net result was a 22.2% devaluation of the property.

If this book gave you a few chuckles, give it to a friend. Should you be lucky and have more than one friend, additional copies may be obtained online.

Uncle Boudreaux's notes on the Strip Center:

Item	**1985 J. Shopper Valuation**	**1987 N.Y. Buyer Valuation**
Cost of Center	$1,000,000	$1,000,000
Cost to our New York Buyer:		$1,000,000
Appraised Value (at 8.3% return)	$1,000,000	$752,381
Loan amount	$800,000	
(Sweetheart loan)		$800,000
Capital Investment	$200,000	$200,000
Income:		
Rental Income (70% occupied)	$140,000	$140,000
Expense:		
Operating Expense	$60,000	$60,000
Net Operating Income	$80,000	$80,000
Note Payment on Loan	$86,487	$86,487
Interest Expense approx.	$80,000	$80,000
Depreciation Expense	$48,387	$24,270
Profit or (Loss)	($48,387)	($32,258)
Loss applied against Other Income	($48,387)	0
Tax Saving from paper losses	$23,258	0
After Tax Cash Flow	$16, 738	($6,487)
Return to Jacque Shopper	8.3%	
Return to Byall Means' Buyer		minus (3.2%)

ABOUT THE AUTHOR

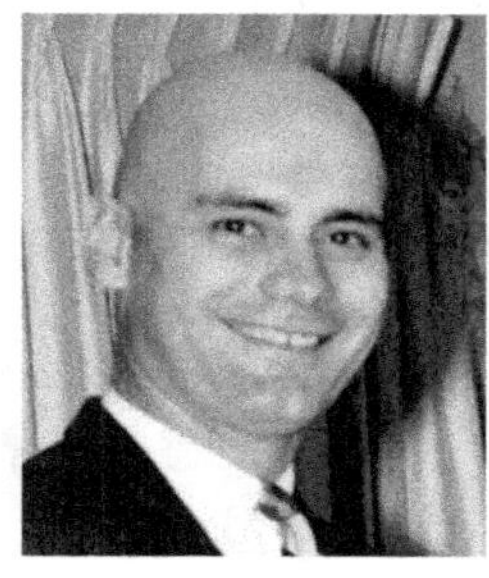

George Marti joined the Navy as a radio operator during World War II. Later, he studied chemical engineering and graduated from of Ohio State University. As a certified professional engineer, he worked in the Far East as the Managing Director of sales for Infilco, Inc. where he negotiated directly with Ministerial and Presidential foreign officials.

He was a native of Warren, Ohio and longtime resident of Covington, Louisiana. He cultivated a wonderful sense of humor and inspired many people on the philosophy of life.

After five years working in Hong Kong, China, he returned home to the USA and started several successful businesses in mud logging, oil and gas investment, marine cleaning, pharmaceuticals, real estate, and land development. He engineered and built several neighborhoods and complexes in the New Orleans and North Shore area including LaCombe Harbor, Sailboat Bay Apartments, and Madisonville on The Lake. He was an avid tennis player and at one time, ranked 7th in the Southern Senior Singles.

His love of knowledge propelled his curiosity of how systems, society, and government influence our lives. He authored the "Pierre LeBlanc" books, "The Great Crash" and "Cover Up" as a manifesto to explain how the 1986 tax law affected millions of Americans.

www.ingramcontent.com/pod-product-compliance
Lightning Source LLC
Chambersburg PA
CBHW060950050726
47592CB00003B/1180

* 9 7 8 0 6 9 2 5 9 5 2 2 0 *